I Do

I Do

Mystic Love Poems

Shilpa Sandesh & Charlz dela Cruz

PARTRIDGE
A Penguin Random House Company

To order additional copies of this book, contact
Partridge India
000 800 10062 62
orders.india@partridgepublishing.com

www.partridgepublishing.com/india

Index:

1. Possessor Of The Flame-
    © Shilpa Sandesh & Charlz dela Cruz 1

2. A fragment – © Charlz dela Cruz................................. 3

3. As They Lie Beneath The Starry Sky-
    © Shilpa Sandesh... 5

4. The Last Petal- © Shilpa Sandesh 7

5. The Mystic Chants- © Shilpa Sandesh....................... 8

6. This is how I sought her- © Charlz dela Cruz.............10

7. The Two Elegiac Souls- © Shilpa Sandesh 13

8. A Promise To My Soul- © Shilpa Sandesh 15

9. Our Wedding In The Garden Of Hesperides-
    © Shilpa Sandesh...16

10. I spell your name- © Charlz Dela Cruz 18

11. The Platonic Mates- © Shilpa Sandesh 20

12. Destiny Rewritten- © Shilpa Sandesh 22

13. Up There, In The Celestial Sphere-
    © Shilpa Sandesh... 23

14. By the light of the Moon- © Charlz dela Cruz 25

15. Undefined- © Shilpa Sandesh 27

16. My Quest Ends At You….- © Shilpa Sandesh........... 28

17. And The Two Drops Shall Be One….-
    © Shilpa Sandesh... 30

18. I Do Not Blame You- © Charlz dela Cruz.................31

19. The Sorcerer's Slave- © Shilpa Sandesh 33

20. And Again Tomorrow-
© (Shilpa Sandesh & Charlz dela Cruz) 34

21. I Will Open You, Petal By Petal-
© Charlz dela Cruz 35

22. Wedding Of The Souls- © Shilpa Sandesh 37

23. The Tranquil Love- © Shilpa Sandesh 39

24. In Your Eyes, Images Of Me- © Shilpa Sandesh 40

25. You are the poem- © Charlz dela Cruz...................... 41

26. We Would Live The Afterlife- © Shilpa Sandesh 43

27. Step Into My Withered Dreams-
© Shilpa Sandesh 44

28. My love….- © Charlz dela Cruz 45

29. Too Much Of You Within Me- © Shilpa Sandesh 47

30. You Are All That Matters- © Shilpa Sandesh 48

31. Mirrors- © Charlz dela Cruz 49

32. Blessed I Would Be….Merry I Would Be-
© Shilpa Sandesh 51

33. The Forbidden Prison Of Ice- © Shilpa Sandesh 53

34. My Beloved- © Charlz dela Cruz 55

35. You And I- © Shilpa Sandesh 57

36. What Is Love Like?- ©
(Shilpa Sandesh & Charlz dela Cruz) 58

37. The song of your voice- © Charlz dela Cruz 60

38. Like Your Shadow, Till Eternity- © Shilpa Sandesh .. 62

39. I Would Be The Demon's Feast- © Shilpa Sandesh ... 64

40. I am yours- © Charlz dela Cruz 66

41. The Hour To Be One Is Here- © Shilpa Sandesh 68

42. Let Our Love Forever Be….- © Shilpa Sandesh 69

43. Locked Up In Eden- © Charlz dela Cruz 70

44. As I Be Your Aphrodite- © Shilpa Sandesh 72

45. Without Being Together- © Shilpa Sandesh.............. 73

46. Eyes- © Charlz dela Cruz 74

47. The Mirth Of Love- © Shilpa Sandesh 76

48. The Timeless Ardent Sparks-
© (Shilpa Sandesh & Charlz dela Cruz) 77

49. If one day- © Charlz dela Cruz.................................. 79

50. The Pleading- © Shilpa Sandesh 81

51. Running Solitary- © Shilpa Sandesh......................... 82

52. I Adore You To Pieces- © Charlz dela Cruz............... 83

53. I Am Your Book's Last Page- © Shilpa Sandesh 86

54. The Blood Moon….Your Message Of Love-
© Shilpa Sandesh... 88

55. Poems are little accidents- © Charlz dela Cruz 89

56. From Across The Seas- © Shilpa Sandesh 90

57. It's Beautiful- © Shilpa Sandesh............................... 92

58. When I miss you- © Charlz dela Cruz 93

59. When Souls In Love Talk- © Shilpa Sandesh............ 95

60. You've Won Me Again- © Shilpa Sandesh................. 97

61. Dear Chatterbox- © Charlz dela Cruz...................... 98

62. The Longing- © Shilpa Sandesh 99

63. I Am Yours- © Shilpa Sandesh................................ 100

64. I carry your tears- © Charlz dela Cruz 101

65. Sometimes All I Wish- © Shilpa Sandesh 103

66. You Are My Salvation….- © Shilpa Sandesh........... 104

67. You are divine- © Charlz dela Cruz...........................105

68. Our Perennial Love- © Shilpa Sandesh.....................107

69. Waiting……..Still- © Shilpa Sandesh 109

70. The Gravity Of Your Love- © Shilpa Sandesh 110

71. Only time- © Charlz dela Cruz 112

72. The Night's Mumbling Heart- © Shilpa Sandesh.....114

73. Lovers' Rhapsody- © Shilpa Sandesh 115

74. Our Voices- © Shilpa Sandesh 117

75. Our Love© Charlz dela Cruz 119

76. You, I And The String Of Pearls-
© Shilpa Sandesh..121

77. Let Me….Let Me Be….- © Shilpa Sandesh 123

78. I Need You……..- © Shilpa Sandesh.......................125

79. Little Conversation- © Charlz dela Cruz 127

80. The Sound Of Your Voice- © Shilpa Sandesh 129

81. All The Love Within Me- © Shilpa Sandesh........... 130

82. Our Voices, Our Lyrics, Our Odes-
© Shilpa Sandesh...131

83. Spells Need Energy- © Charlz Dela Cruz 132

84. I Have Loved You Since Time Immemorial-
© Shilpa Sandesh...133

85. Wake Up, Good Morrow To You!-
© Shilpa Sandesh... 134

86. Oh Mine……..- © Shilpa Sandesh...........................135

87. Beneath The Moon….- © Shilpa Sandesh 137

88. Street Rat- © Charlz dela Cruz................................ 138

89. To Meet Thy Élan Vital- © Shilpa Sandesh 140

90. Us Together- © (Shilpa Sandesh & Charlz dela Cruz) ... 141

91. The Eloquent Dusk- © Shilpa Sandesh 142

92. Sweet Phantom Of The Night-
© Charlz dela Cruz 144

93. Perseverance En Amour- © Shilpa Sandesh............. 145

94. You……...- © Shilpa Sandesh 147

95. Let There Be No Regrets!- © Shilpa Sandesh........... 149

96. Beauty Is An Illusion- © Charlz dela Cruz 151

97. The Eternal Embrace- © Shilpa Sandesh 153

98. The Whole Of You- © Shilpa sandesh 154

99. Till Our Absolute Exultation….-
© Shilpa Sandesh... 155

100. Powerful Spells- © Charlz dela Cruz 157

101. Wishing My Enchanter….A Happy Birthday!-
© Shilpa Sandesh... 159

102. When We shall Meet….- © Shilpa Sandesh 161

103. If- © Charlz dela Cruz.. 163

104. Steps To Thee….- © Shilpa Sandesh 165

105. Today And Every Morning….- © Shilpa Sandesh 166

106. The Seeker Of The Seer….- © Shilpa Sandesh......... 168

107. There Is A Rose- © Charlz dela Cruz 171

108. Cupid's Delight- © Shilpa Sandesh 172

109. Our Castle In The Air….- © Shilpa Sandesh 173

110. Mysticism- © Shilpa Sandesh................................... 175

111. How Your Body Moves- © Charlz dela Cruz............ 177

112. One More Day- © Shilpa Sandesh 179

113. Pain….- © Shilpa Sandesh 180

114. My Spell….- © Shilpa Sandesh 183

115. Laugh- © Charlz dela Cruz 184

116. As Long As The Night Sways….-
© Shilpa Sandesh...186

117. Your Verses….Your Words….My Eyes-
© Shilpa Sandesh...187

118. My Precious….Good Morning To You!-
© Shilpa Sandesh...188

119. Before there were flowers- Charlz dela Cruz 189

120. A Song For You….- © Shilpa Sandesh 191

121. Would You Stay With Me Still?- © Shilpa Sandesh...193

122. How do I appease your beauty?-
© Charlz dela Cruz 195

123. I Am Restless- © Shilpa Sandesh 196

124. Together Forever- © Shilpa Sandesh 198

125. My Wizard….- © Shilpa Sandesh 199

126. I Do….- © (Shilpa Sandesh & Charlz dela Cruz) 200

Preface

It is true that soul has its own language. And when the souls speak, connections are made, the strings from heaven get tied together to fill the expressions of the soul with magic. Bask on this beatific journey of two souls which have met after countless lives and deaths, finally to unite in the unceasing bond of seraphic love.........

Possessor Of The Flame

I have loved you from some distant past,
When my body, filled with dark matter,
Sought for the true light....
Lost and broken, I dashed against the night,
One by one, I plucked the stars,
Searching for the meaning,
But they were found wanting,
Just meaningless glows,
Empty shimmers,
Until,
Until I beheld your vision,
Then everything that the world knows, about Love,
Everything that the eyes adore, about Beauty,
Ceased to exist,
Because............

Somewhere, in the unfrequented lands,
A flame fluttered,
Trapped in a lamp,
A lamp so beauteous,
like a world of glass walls,
With material pomp, glitters, wishes,
Temporary grandeur and vainglory,
All together violating the flame,

While it still yelled, prayed and yelled,
The flame,
I,
I awaited,
Looking up on that small circular exit,
I prayed to be pulled up,
When the wolves of fallacy and perfidy ambushed me,
My faith in your coming, kept me alive,
And here,
I stand finally sought, as my saviour's desire and fancy,

So, Oh mine....
If I be the light, that drowned the darkness inside of you,
Then you are the preserver of this flame,
The possessor of this flame.........

A fragment

What was love like
        To a soul misunderstood
By every fiber of humanity?

Love was nothing like poetry
It was only like a fragment of her breath
A mere moisture that spreads into the open air
That I hungrily chase with my lips

It was nothing more than my fingers
Trying to grasp a soul-ful of body
More surreal than myself, I touch
But can never hold

Because a soul can never understand a body
Just as a body will never relate to a soul
Because only a soul can understand
Another soul

It was not love
Not anything like it
Because true souls do not care about love
I only know how to talk with stars
And wish for her eyes
Because even amidst the cruel world
Souls only know how to dream

And so I dream
And dreaming
Dreaming

Dissolving.

And how does it feel
To lose this Friend?

Dear One, it is
Like having a shard of glass
That slowly traces your every curvature, and every line
To teach a soul
How to bleed.

As They Lie Beneath The Starry Sky

Words I have written,
The reverences proclaimed,
All appear barren,
Worthless and in vain;

Magic searched my words,
Or my expressions yearned enchantment,
The dilemma is no more,
The divination discovers the core;

I wonder whether I digressed,
Or the magic drifted from its course,
Poetry personifies me,
Under the wizard's spell I shall stay;

The joy knows no bounds,
The magnetism or an illusion,
A power or fascination,
This allure is so profound;

A connection of the souls,
In quest for each other,
Words and the spell,
Are finally together;

The pursual ends,
Incertitude resolves,
Let the two laugh, forgetting the sighs,
As they lie beneath the starry sky.

The Last Petal

The hymns,
   The chants,
The psalm of affection,
And the carol of love.......
Engrossed in his anticipation,
Mind theorizing the perception,
Soul ruminating the feelings,
And heart,
Heart innervating the pleasures;

My eyes catch sight of a marigold,
Blooming yellow and orange,
Fifty beauteous petals,
First pluck.......He loves me,
Another pluck.....He loves me more,
Another pluck......His love is bounteous,
Pluck.....Plucks......the last petal reached,
As the fingers advance,
To pick that final petiole,
The warm breaths and a whisper,
Brushes against my ear,
And in his faintly seductive voice says,
"The last petal,
The last petal says,
I love you infinitely!"

The Mystic Chants

A moment of tranquillity,
 When darkness rules,
Beneath the full moon's light,
Our souls leave our bodies,
Yours and mine,
Amidst the green valleys of Machu Picchu,
A Mayan from the pre-classical era,
Strumming the huge Heuheutl drum,
As a group of the tribes danced,
To the Mayan ritual chants,
We held our hands,
As if to be a part,
Of the customs of the deities colel ek tun,
Or colel cab or may be colel peten,
A glance upon the sky,
And there it was,
The huge fire ball,
Like a call,
And our souls flew around,
Like consuming the energy,
Letting the light sink in,
Percolate every single pore,
And we dance,
To the tunes of mystic chants,
Like being one,
One,
One in the Seraphic trance,

I Do

Two souls, One soul,
One soul, two souls,
And we part,
To resume our conscious selves,
Until we hear again,
The Mystic Mayan Chants,
And be One again and again and again......

This is how I sought her

"Seek and you shall find
Knock and the door shall be
opened" -Matthew 7:7, Holy Bible

This is how I sought her
That dream from a thousand light years:

I patiently knocked on a million doors
Creatures appeared, brute, bestial
Thus also a million times
Did I close my own door

And as I prowled the streets of August
Feeling defeated by the night, and murdered by the cold
I saw these little fragments, shining, mysterious
One by one, I put the pieces together
And then --- and then
Amidst the haunting darkness and the rough winds
Amidst shattering dreams and bleeding hearts
The fragments lit up, the skies opened
as if to swallow humanity
And there --- she stood --- smiling,
her hand filling the gaps
Between my fingers

Suddenly, everything found its meaning
Rocks, metals, colors --- everything
Fire finally lifted itself back into the sun
While the rain made its way back into the sea
Because there she was
And now, here she is --- Beauty, Innocent, Divine

(Ufff)

Poetry
Poetry made flesh
Her lips, finely shaped in silent verses
While she moves with the rhyme
Of blooming flowers
And her voice, oh her voice carries in itself
The distinct softness of the ever sweet
Violin
And if you should know about her soul
Then I should tell you
That it is as the Nile
Vast and infinite --- only deeper
Like her eyes

While I, breathless
I look at her
My heart, pounding
Drowning, in the beauty

Of her existence

(Ufff)

Is it love then? You ask

Answer: No
Of course not
For love is everywhere, except here
Because everything that the rotten world knows about love
Has not reached this place

Listen: This is something more holy
Too holy
That no skin shall be touched
Too holy
Even for the gods.

The Two Elegiac Souls

What would it be like,
    To be a poet's muse,
Poetry ponders,
An inspiration and an impulse,
And with words to be fused;

Spellbound is the verse,
By the magic's charm,
Or is the spell ensnared,
By the Poesy's raptures?

To portray this beguiling bond,
There are no words to expound,
Companionship is too unjust,
Inadequate to call it Love,
What could then it be,
Only the two can tell;

The poetry is touched,
By the magic's wizardry,
A touch so celestial,
Through the winds and moon and stars;

Words take a leap,
Poetry becomes a song,
The song becomes a story,
To be lived forever,
by the two elegiac souls.

A Promise To My Soul

I had promised to my soul,
That I would cry no more,
But I am sorry,
The sobs just don't stop....
The tears just won't stop.....

A heart that was, is still a heart,
It's not a prey,
On which you aim your dart,
It hurts, it scars,
And it leaves me wounded,
And for a moment I feel,
I feel like that fairy tale princess,
A princess, trapped behind the golden bars!

Let me stand in the rain,
So that I wouldn't know I'm crying,
And no tear shall remain a tear,
Every drop shall turn into rain;

Oh but my soul!
I promise I won't cry,
I would cry no more,
And I would fight the tears,
To keep the promise forevermore....

Our Wedding
In The Garden Of Hesperides

The holy path has been laid,
  In the garden of the Hesperides,
Where Zeus accepted Hera,
The altar has been set,
Under the tree bearing golden apples,
Where dressed in a Greek wedding gown,
I shall walk towards you,
On the path sheathed in roses,
White and red,
Tough it is to wait,
To see those gleaming eyes,
As they would look into mine,
While I would take the divine stride,
That moment, everything would halt,
Nothing we would see or know or feel,
But You and I and the vows,
Such would be the aurora,
Of the new life,
Life that has no age,
No end and no bounds,
But just the vows of togetherness,
In joys and the sorrows,
A wedding that the Gods and the Goddesses,
Shall mention in the sacred lore,

I Do

There was a union of souls,
Amidst the butterflies and fireflies,
Fairies and elves and nymphs,
Our Wedding in the garden of Hesperides...........

I spell your name

I spell your name
Not like a-b-c
Because I spell your name
I spell your name, like this:

From your soft hands shall rise, black smoke
Of voodoo magick
An endless weaving of angelic curses
You shall always find me, in every corner
Of your mind, in the deepest shadow
Crafting (uni)verses in your name
Breathe, and I become your breath
Think, for I am your thoughts
Sleep, and I dream
You are bound not to understand
The language of the body, nor the heat of one's skin
Nor what it means to be touched
Until my whole body, dips
Into your soul

But because you are
My innumerable desires
Because you are
My numberless dreams

I Do

Know this:
For one strand of your hair
I would snatch away
The silver of the moon

I spell your name

I spell your name

I spell your name.

The Platonic Mates

L ove....
Is it all that is?
Or
Is it the most beauteous?

Love is a mere confession,
A feeling, an aggression,
Like anguish, like melancholy,
Feelings dominated by wisdom,
Or by folly;

It is but something more,
Something prepossessing,
Above all the allure,
Something graceful and aesthetic,
Miles from imprudence and inanity;

Mind dwells deeper,
The shovel of undefined inquisitiveness,
Digs into abysmal depths;

Can there be a touch, without a touch?

Yes,
An embrace without an embrace,
A kiss without the meeting of the lips,

Entangling fingers from seas apart,
Where the two can still hear,
The beating of each others heart;

So Oh Wizard,
If you sense a presence,
An aura, an invisible semblance,
It's the wish, a dream,
An ethereal beam,
Rising from my soul,
In search of its true master,
And in your soul,
It shall meet.

Destiny Rewritten

On the pages,
Of the book called Life,
Where a prolonged past lies,
With an abundance of miseries,
And extinct smiles,
I step onto the coliseum of contemporaneous;

As I begin to perform my song of sorrows,
From among the audience,
Audience, the guilty, the liable of my anguish,
A cheer distracts,
The hail that changed the lyrics of my song,
And from melancholy and woes,
Delirium ruled my vocal chords;

And soon I realized,
There you were,
The sole symbol of solace,
In the gaggle of the symbols of disharmony,
And I stood singing, smitten,
I knew,
Lines on my palm were being recast,
My destiny was being rewritten.........

Up There, In The Celestial Sphere

An eruption of zillion infernos,
A sea of flames heightens and grows,
Every pore opening to the magnetic air,
The body, a holocaust of antagonism,
Washed with the torrent of seraphic blaze,
Freed from the qualms, now clean and bare;

The ardent minims awakened,
Charged with the zealous fervor,
Bombarding in our bodies,
Across the bones and veins,
The volcano of ardor flares up,
The soul exits,
Leaving the numbness behind;

The two frames,
With rapturous yellow flames,
Are the two souls,
Who met for ages,
And were parted,
In their endeavors to unite,
But the devotion never died,
With every travail, every stab,
The love therein multiplied,
The yearning of the two determined hearts,

Intensified,
The wheel of time,
Changed its pace,
And before their bodies,
Their souls met;

This flame, this fire,
Forever would stay,
Even if the wrath of time,
Makes mountains erode to sand,
The glaciers melt into sea,
And the sea evaporates into the air,
Our two souls,
Would stay one forever,
Up there,
In the celestial sphere........

By the light of the Moon

By the light of the Moon
My heartbeats
Sending you morse codes
In a dialect you alone can understand

By the light of the Moon
I see dreams, mesh
With the fibres of reality
Stars smiling at each other; and blue roses, laughing

By the light of the Moon
I whisper my wish in the air
And I inhale you
Because I feel you everywhere

By the light of the Moon
Now I understand
Why amidst the dissolving universe
God created the stars

By the light of the Moon
My chest opens, and my soul shoots off
Up to the Moon, and back
To you

My Saint, all these, and more
While you sing
By the light of the Moon
While you write
By the light of the Moon.

Undefined

If tears can tell it all,
Then I would cry whole night,

If smiles can be a proof,
I would laugh like mads for you,

It is not what,
The world might perceive,
Because it is,
Miles ahead,
From what everyone can see,

Divinity has been sought for long,
It has now been achieved,
I wonder what this longing is,
Oh wizard,
Make me at ease....

My Quest Ends At You....

H eartache....
Catastrophe, miseries,
Tribulations,

Exuberance,
Elation, vivacity,
Merriment,

A journey,
I sustained,
From far away to far away,
I wrote twinge, afflictions,
And heap of throes;

An excursion that began,
when I first opened my eyes,
And soon a whirl it was,
A ride from pampers and coddles,
To false attractions and falser desires;

An angel watched,
From far afield earth,
I had read about the God sent,
They have eyes like gems,
A smile like Messiah's,
Sacrosanct expressions,
And cherubic accent;

I wondered,
"Who be the blessed ones,
Whom the angel would meet?"
Least did I know,
My ride of hitch and spins,
Was turning into a joyride,
Of supreme grace,
For,
The angel, You, found me,
And glorified I am,
As I look into your eyes,
Your divine glare permeates the whole of me,
And drink the expressions,
Of your ethereal face,
And,
My quest ends at you........

And The Two Drops Shall Be One....

We have been that drop,
	Which once traversed,
with the other drops,
Into the caravan of love angels,
Flowing from galaxies to galaxies,
In the vast universe;
But there was one more Satan,
And we, the drop, was split,
And thrown into the two hemispheres;
Only we know what it is to yearn,
For we are one body one soul,
Without eachother, we aren't whole;
A day there shall be,
That moment shall be,
When the two drops,
Shall again be One.........

I Do Not Blame You

Sometimes, when a beautiful soul is too overwhelmed
By its own love, by its own divinity
It becomes blind...

I do not blame you
Not your sadness that makes my body dissipate, slowly
Into the ripe air
Nor your sweet self suddenly shunned into silence
Silence so deafening you did not hear my heart drop
A hundred feet from the ground

I do not blame you
Because perhaps you do not see me clearly
Perhaps we do not really see each other eye to eye
For I am lost in the curvature of your eyes
That I am more than soul now than
skin, muscles, and bones
But go ahead and be mad; do it, be sad
And I bleed

It is you who do not know what you
mean to me, what you do to me
Keep this in your mind: I am not in love with you
I alone am not in love with you
But every cell in my body is
And my soul, my poor soul, it is your existence
That defines my soul

Dear Saint, if I only had one power, one wish to make
By that same light of the Moon, I would steal your lips
With my lips
While you, and the whole world
Sleep.

The Sorcerer's Slave

Amazed are the verses,
By an intense idiosyncrasy
A sudden spasmodic variation,
Autumn turns to spring,
Heartaches into cheer and contentment,
Can the world be,
So enticing and resplendent,
As it now seems to me,

This is the aura I sought,
No money can buy it,
No beauty can lure,
Let me merge with the seer,
I am the sorcerer's slave,
Make me lose these breaths,
Let me dare the maze,
The path perpetual, unknown,
Across the cosmic shores,
As I don't belong
To this unjust existence anymore!

And Again Tomorrow....

I love you more
From the deepest depths of my heart, I adore you
From head to toe, to the tips of your fingernails,
down to the last molecule in your body
Because I love you more....

I miss you more,
From across the deepest of the oceans,
Which my soul traverses day and night,
On my heart's command,
To have a glimpse of you,
It defies the spirited cyclones,
And the stifling black blizzards,
While it's wings ache and crave for death,
It glides a thousand miles,
To see,
To absorb, to imbibe your divine smile,
Till it's another journey,
Because,
Because I miss you more....

And there goes love
Courting the moon, swallowing the sun
That even missing makes love move ---
A fleeting, beautiful sorrow
That I shall love you more, and more
Again tomorrow.

I Will Open You,
Petal By Petal

I will open you, petal by petal
Slowly, amidst exchanging breaths
Feel my fingers send ripples down your skin
Tracing constellations made of desires, erupting
Urges

Watch me surrender my soul
To every inch of your splendor
While I examine the pages of your body
Soft, glowing, and infinite
Every pore, every curve
Nothing will be left untouched

Feel how my lips write my devotions on your naked self
The blunt confessions of a soul, in lust with divinity
And make your body tremble, with
your already trembling lips
For I will eat you down, until your words falter
Until your sighs learn to pray

And beneath the curious moon, and the shy burning stars
I will look straight into your eyes, bask
in every expression you make
As I stretch you open, with my hard wicked body

Digging in to you --- slowly, passionately
And without mercy

While love, that strange mysterious love, melts
Into our sweat
Then I will hold you, pull you, closest
Oh, my most sacred --- now gasping, relished
Yet we still need
To inhale each other

With tears in our eyes, we turn our soft murmurs
Into deafening moans
Moans that conjure the Soul of God
(Because the holiest moans can only come
From two imperfect souls, meshed
In prayer)
And then nothing --- nothing but ecstatic bliss
And the desire to be enlightened
Shall be
No more

For nothing will remain
But the combined scent of two souls
One shared breath, and a dreamless sleep

For once, let me show your body
What it really means
To be touched:
Like a moth, caressed
By fire.

Wedding Of The Souls

Years have passed,
  Seasons bygone,
In benumbing winters,
And the zealous summers,
They searched and searched,
Their souls' rightful owners;

The moment sprung,
One fine day,
The two met,
Magic and Poetry,
And the path was laid,
For their holy walk;

Flowers were sheathed,
For the divine aisle,
Where demons and Gods,
And the spirits stood,
Blessings treasured,
For countless years,
Were showered upon,
The two souls;

The Moon was the priest,
Who united the hearts,

Which fluttered for long,
In the pangs and stings,
In throes and twinge;

The Poesy said,
To her beloved soul
"My search Oh seer,
Ends here,
I was on a quest,
Frisked here and there,
Here you stood,
Casting your spell,
Bound I am now,
To walk along,
Whether a stride
In the alluring heaven
Or a tread,
In the thorny hell"!

The Tranquil Love

Oh light of my life,
        A poetess I am,
I originate from your love,
I smile, I weep, I laugh,
When I write,
Because as I do so,
My physical self, with a pen and a paper,
Is a mere illusion to the one who espies me,
For my inner self merges,
With the scenario in creation,
The schema wherein,
Are you and I,
And the quarantine silence,
The silence that is,
The unspoken, the tranquil love........

In Your Eyes, Images Of Me

A dry leaf,
Turned into a blossoming orange,
Golden and yellow, like a maple bliss,
Smiles long gone,
Returned in full bloom,
Where the sorrows become joys,
Stones become gems,
I see all of these,
As I look into your eyes,
For there stays forever,
Myself and all the images of me...............

You are the poem

You are the poem
   My eyes have been dying to read, repeatedly
Without end
But it cannot be told how your words strum
The rusty heartstrings inside me
For when I flipped through your page
And my eyes met the soul that owns them
I could not believe my eyes
Because even my eyes could not believe themselves:

In your stillness, my body trembles
Knees go weak and drowning
Yet I taste every line and crevice of your words
Just as how I intend to eat the edges of your lips
And when you talk, my mind goes blank
While my heart, as if made of flowers
As if commanded by your whispers
Opens its petals to your golden rays
But not knowing how to close back
Not knowing how to keep your voice
silent, and locked up within
I explode into your dreams --- dreams that gather
Like pools in your eyes
With all your desires now flowing
In my veins
And this, my love, is what I call
Life

Because believe me:
No star has yet fallen
No sun has ever risen
Into this, and whatever
Will be

But if you should know
How a soul dies
You only need to take back your words
While I read, while I believe ---
Simply, with your hand
Close
My eyes.

We Would Live The Afterlife

They stood seas apart,
    Gazing at the celestial sphere,
He looks at the moon of the night,
While she stares at the evening moon,
Bodies across the distances,
But souls so near;

If it be the rule,
Of a bond undefined,
As rays define the permanence of the Sun,
As the rains define, presence of the clouds,
So does his untouched touch,
To her flowing hair,
Defines the existence of the wind;

The vigor of this yearning,
Is beyond the sensuous touch,
Be it not, just the moments extant,
Be it not, just the urge,
We would live the afterlife,
As then the souls would merge!

Step Into My Withered Dreams

Let me Oh love!
      Let me see you for once,
For once in my barren dreams,
My barren dreams of sorrowful streams,
The sorrowful streams of demons and screams,
Screams, which awaken me every night,
Every night from a nightmarish sleep,
Sleep......
I wish to sleep.......
I wish to dream.....
To see that blaze, that seraphic beam,
The doors are open,
They would always be,
For the one, the one who is You,
So reprieve not my Beloved,
Step into my withered dreams,
I await that divine sheen,
Step into my withered dreams........

My love....

M y love, you stand in beauty
Amidst the fluctuating universe
Like a beautiful flowerpot, by the window
On a rainy day
Your unassuming beauty, defying
Gravity
That before your soul, my heart
Rises, from the pale and muddy ground
To the galaxies in your eyes
At once, my heart leaps
At once, my heart climbs
Your ladder, saying
There is my home
There is my home

My love, let me adore you
Because I adore you deeply, in love and in lust
And both, divine
Let me drink you like water
Lick your skin with a tongue of fire, quenching flesh
Let me inhale you like air
Quick to the touch, erratic to the bones
Let me feel you, sweetly fill you, everywhere
Or let my soul be made of earth
So I would hammer it down, into pieces
And send them to your shore, that
impatiently waits for me

Or deny me this sacred adoration
Deny me my begging pleas
And see me only as who I am:
Everyday
Watch me bleed with every sunset, saying
You are my home
You are my home.

Too Much Of You Within Me

I wish you could see into my mind,
And peep into my inner self,
But let me tell you,
You won't see a thing,
Because your view would be obstructed,
By too much of you,
Too much of you within me!

You Are All That Matters

I have been the destiny's
Favourite child,
When karma ruled my being,
Life's all aspects, I seem to have seen,
A moment after numerous miseries,
I lifted a step,
To walk on the sea,
Knowing that no one,
Has tread on the blue spread,
I knew I would drown,
But still, I was urged to stride ahead,
And just when I was to fall,
And be one with the sea,
You pulled me back,
Like an angel, emerging from a bright light,
My seer,
You are for me,
My everything,
Without you, there's nothing,
A fear grips me, numbing my entire self,
And I shrink to become a fate's tiny elf,
To say I need you, are just three aligned words,
My Wizard, I love you,
You are all that matters,
Leave me not, forget me not,
For then,
I would be no more...........

Mirrors

M irrors have their own magic
As everyday they cut themselves
Into your reflection
Such is the life of all mirrors:
Everyday, they measure you from head to toe
Everyday, they try to shape your beauty
Everynight, they dream the impossible dream
And soon they break, just as how hearts are torn
Because true beauty cannot be contained in a mirror
Simply because true beauty is not made of reflections
But do not be sad, Dear One
Because you are the joy of mirrors
And to break for the love of you
Is the dream of all mirrors

Sometimes, I wish I were a mirror
So I could show you such love
But my poor soul has nothing to do with mirrors
I cannot reflect light, neither am I
A gleam in your eye
But I know how to break a soul,
and be like all broken mirrors

For I am already broken

My Saint, I have loved you
Even before I learned to notice the
curves of a woman's body
I have loved you in the pages of my diary,
even before I learned how to write
And I will always love you, I will always love you
Even if your gentle lips tell my heart
To stop beating

My Joy, each time you look in the mirror
Know that you alone have the pieces of my soul
All in love with you, happy, blessed
Ready to be broken again

Truly, mirrors have nothing to do with my love
Because I am not made of glass
And because I have loved you long before
Any mirror did.

Blessed I Would Be....
Merry I Would Be

M y soul,
My true self,
Hysterical or insane,
Or in a frenzied state,
I know not;

But I know this:

When your heart weeps,
I hear the shrill,
Of my soul in pain,
And it bows to surrender,
Without any whims,
Or whims undefined,
Without any dispositions,
Or worldly gains;

In the deepest depths,
Of my inner self,
I feel an ache,
A thousand pines,
Leaving me still,
Unstirring but serene,
Stable but lifeless;

My soul then peeps,
Into his divine self,
And in that vast ocean of love,
I feel as tiny as an elf;
And then a treble,
A cacophonous sound,
And all that I could hear,
Oh my wicked destiny,
Burn me with thousand fires,
Dig into me a thousand swords,
Tie me with thorns and ropes,
But in turn,
Give my restless soul,
just one chance,
A moment,
That moment,
The touch of divinity,
Blessed I would be,
Merry I would be....

The Forbidden Prison Of Ice

I am the iceberg,
In the frozen lands of nowhere,
I waited,
Amidst the blizzards and the snow flurries,
I stood stiffened under the spell of the ice,
Like a humming bird,
Imprisoned behind the bleak bars;

The moment arrived,
A sudden wind of warmth,
Melted my prison's peripheral surface,
And I saw you riding on a silver horse,
Like a prince of the Newfound land,
I see you still,
Striding towards me,
To unlock the doors of this dungeon,
I am blue with cold,
My breaths loosing pace with time,
Approach me soonest I plead, be mine,
I have fallen on my knees,
I can stand no more,
I await your warm embrace,
That would,
Melt me down,

And free I would be,
From what seems to be beauty to the eyes,
From this, which veritably is the
forbidden prison of ice..........

My Beloved

I breathe
The words of my Beloved
They encircle me, round and round
And I inhale them, down
To the densest formation of atoms
In my body

I dance
In the verse of my Beloved
From her flowing rhythm, I bend
And pluck immortality
Because my Beloved writes for me
She writes on my soul

I wander
In the writings of my Beloved
Like some myth
On a secret page of literature
Kept sacred by the gods
Born from her lips, and caressed
By her hands

I sing
Every line penned by my Beloved
Like perfect constellations
Set in the sky
How sweetly she pens

Her letters to me:
They carry the glow
Of infinite moons

And I write
Because
She exists
I write
Because
Of my Beloved.

You And I

Songs......
I would hum,
While I gaze at the moon,

Words....
I would scrawl,
Imagining your glimpse,

Dreams....
I would fancy,
You besides me

Breaths....
I would breathe,
Your fragrance, your incense that be,

My enchanter,
My life, my soul,
Here I stand,
Forever I will,
My arms widespread,
As I wait for you!

What Is Love Like?

What is love like?
  Asks a leaf
Falling, to kiss the soil;

An obsession of touch,
A compulsion of intimacy,
And souls in beauteous clutch;

Or is it a certain kind of wonder,
That holds two stars apart,
Yet keeps their gaze, upon each other,
So that one day they would fall,
Fall as all raindrops do,
Together;

A bewilderment it is,
A whirlwind,
With the molecules of enamored flames,
In between two hemispheres,
Befuddled as to where to go,
Urging the two hemispheres,
To come closer, to be one,
To make a sphere,
The aphrodisiac sphere;

I Do

Then closer they move,
And one shall they be,
For the leaf and the soil have,
unknowingly loved each other,
Even before the stars were made,
Because they are one sap, one breath,
Same soul, intertwined,
So the leaf simply falls,
Back
To its home;

Home it is,
For that tenacious bond,
A silken string, where in are
The rosaries of devotion,
And two souls' pious vows,
Love it is so incessantly pure,
That even the Time would halt to bow....

Shilpa Sandesh & Charlz dela Cruz

The song of your voice

The song of your voice...
A perfect combustion of notes, smoothly scaled
To the size of my heart
It measures my every molecule
Hypnotizes every cell
It burns my body, apart
(To fill me with music ---
The music of your lips)

And I hear your songs
From those same words exhaled from your mouth
I eat your voice like a cherry and digest it
To its last fleeting note
While my heart flutters down your feet, my soul sways
And my world dances
To your beat

Because when you sing, the sun sets
For the smile of the crescent moon
Lost eyes of strangers lock with another
And all flowers swoon
When you sing, white lilies cascade
down from the sky like waterfalls
And mountains leap to the stars
When you sing, words become alive
And music finds its meaning

I Do

My love, sing
For I am born from your breath
Invade me with your words, turn me into your music
And let me taste infinity
On your lips
For once, make me immortal

Because you sing me
To the moon
And only the song of your voice
Can sing me
To life.

Like Your Shadow, Till Eternity

My Soul....
Hiked across the densest of the dense woods,
Swam athwart the deepest of the deep seas,
Flew beyond the highest of the blue spread above;

Exasperated and broken down,
It was set to collapse;

But then....
A mystical, ambrosial power,
The blissful, Your soul,
Your soul held mine,
And I stirred;

As the world turned me,
Into a heap of hay,
An existence in vain,
A tree which saw,
It's leaves dry,
You My Love,
Emerged like my gardener,
And as you would water me,
Forever tender I would be;

The wait was long,
As long as it could be,
I locked away my love,

Hid in the deepness of my heart,
For now I know,
It was meant to be,
Showered upon none but You;

Oh My Love,

I have known you,
Not since a day or days or months or years,
I have known you,
Since even before I existed,
I am no slave to these breaths,
Nor to this life,
For I would be with you,
Like your shadow,
Till Eternity....

Shilpa Sandesh & Charlz dela Cruz

I Would Be The Demon's Feast

I remember,
We just began our walk,
Hands in hands, on a fiery path,
Where there are no golden maples,
Scattered beneath our steps,
But pines and thorns ornate our ingress,
Into the gates of the Abode of Seraphic Lovers,
We've held each other firm so far,
And my grip fastens with every step;

This walk, which once seemed like an ordeal,
Has now become a gratifying tramp,
Where pines seem as soft as rose petals,
And my bleeding feet seem,
Like being washed with Heaven's nectar;

Leave not my hand,
Let any spell bind you,
Leave not this tread,
For I would forget to walk,
And there would be but just one spell,
One spell that I would master,
A spell that I would cast on myself,
On how to invite the demons,
To feast on me,

And all that would be left for you to see,
Would be some bones, some blood,
And the chains,
Which the demons tied me with........

I am yours

I am yours
Take away my eyes, body, soul
I am yours

Take my eyes
For they were made only for you
That I love you blindly, beyond borders
Biting the stars between my teeth, I jumped off the cliff
Then you held me, and lifted me higher than the sun
Into your blinding brightness

Take my body
Grab it with your skin, take it in your mouth
Swallow me with your hands
And leave your fingerprints on places
You alone can touch

Take my soul
Because the more you take, the more I love
For my soul depends upon you
I feed on your existence

My Saint, you hold my life together
And while other planets revolve aimlessly,
you keep me in your orbit
Where stars are made of dreams, forged
By the gravity of your love

Come fantasies, come music, verses
In the wind of the breeze, in the liquid of the rain
All over me

You are my galaxy
You are my infinity

Take me, please
I am yours
I am yours.

The Hour To Be One Is Here

Embracing bodies,
Blending breaths,
Fingers entwined,
Tenaciously clinching,
The Hour to be one,
Is here....

Let Our Love Forever Be....

M i amor

I am the wall

That stands midst
Hurdles and you,

I am those chants
Which would absorb
All your pain
And give you
Those immortal smiles,

My life Oh love,
Has meaning
Since you happened to me
Amongst all situations of our being
Let our love forever be....

Locked Up In Eden

Locked up in Eden
There was nothing unusual about
serpents that could talk
Or ants that sing and dance
Nothing strange about birds flying from afar,
enjoying the mountains and the seas
While I was busy watering the plants,
or counting shooting stars

I am the first of my specie, perhaps with
the most mistakes in the making
But God is a God of love and alchemy
That from my base imperfections, he took the smoothest
bone He could find, and carved it into perfection
And there, my love, my life --- you rose
As the most beautiful of creation:

You stood, more naked than the mountains
With curvatures, tightly cut
Your body rubbed against mine
And I tasted your sweat that carries the saltiness of the sea
Your eyes taught me why shooting stars keep falling
I knew right there and then:
You are my soul, you are my soul

I was wrong
God never wanted to cage me in a garden

He simply knew from the beginning
That happiness is meant to be shared
And this is the only way to be truly happy
Perhaps this is also the reason why He created everything
And as sewn into the fabric
Of truth:
The whole universe is happy
Everything is sacred
But only true love
Can hold sin
Without fear

Then your words echoed in my ear: "Anything
that comes from the soul is pure
Because everything from the soul is divine."
With this, we held sin like an apple in our hands
And with a bite, and with a smile
The sweetest sin was born
And this be the sin
That freed our souls, that were locked up
In Eden.

As I Be Your Aphrodite

B link of an eye,
And in the Hellenic era,
We alight,
Our love,
So pellucid and bright;

I breathe in the heaven,
Of azure bliss,
An empyrean of dreams,
And eternal rest;

But I wish no more,
Of the glory,
And the pearly gates,
I wing towards You,
My Adonis,
As I be your Aphrodite....

Without Being Together

Walking solitary,
  On the dank coastal sand,
I observe a pair of footsteps,
That accompany mine,
And so I realize,
To be physically together in love,
Is necessary,
But it is not everything,
Because when the love is true,
Deep and profound,
Lovers hold hands without being together,
Lovers kiss each other, without being together,
Lovers feel each others presence, without being together,
Just like,
I am there besides you,
While you drive your car,
Humming our favorite song,
And
You are with me, here,
Walking on the wet beach sand,
Without being with me,
Without us being together.......

Eyes

"The eyes are the windows to the soul"
   At least, this is what they say
Yet nobody can tell how a soul looks like
Or how the blue sea is carried
Inside two still, black eyes
Because they have not seen your eyes
Eyes that speak and grab
Straight where my heart lies

Eyes so deep and penetrating
Light as an unheard whisper
And dark as a beautiful murder
They cut straight through my bones, so beautifully
That I bleed galaxies of love, and silent drips of poems
Because your eyes, they are two blackholes
That define beauty
And they devour me
They swallow my everything, as sweetly
As how you carry the sky in your eyes
And drown the sea in them

While in the firmament between your eyes and mine
Is my heart, beating, on some shore
Measuring your boundless expanse, embracing infinity
And like a flower that opens itself to the sun

I Do

I stretch open myself
To the vastness of your vision:

I make love with your light
I make love with your eyes
I make love with your soul
With my soul in your eyes.

The Mirth Of Love

No mercy shall be sought,
No pity desired,
The two would meld,
Blend like river and the sea,
When fire would rule,
The arch of amour,
And the flames of passion,
Enlighten,
The mirth of Love....

The Timeless Ardent Sparks

The swells and the waves ahead of me,
Seem deliriously euphoric,
As if to pull me, in their ecstatic spree,
Or is it the celestial call,
For the two soul's enamoured jamboree?

It is the pull
Of the flesh
Which also gives me no rest
It comes, haunting
The touch of your head on my chest
And the call for communion
Of souls
Just as skin is made for skin
Lips for lips
Sweat for sweat
So do souls also crave to be touched
So do souls also need to be exploited, and ravaged
Down to the very last drop
So come, my love, in complete submission
Come, as a holy sacrifice, without reservation
For even the smallest crevice will not be left undone
For the bodies shall talk, bones shall
bend, and moans shall sing
Come, like how all fires rise
To join the sun: Burn, and surrender
Everything....

Hither I poise,
Trembling, with a stream within,
Like an inferno of howling passion,
My hands, await to be held by thou,
Come my soul,
Turn this mortality into an immortal zeal,
Let every ounce of me,
Glow with the blaze in thee,
When the two flames, two souls,
Shall burn,
Into a volcano of ecstasy, the Elysian skies would turn,
Paroxysm of lust,
Hasty fondles,
Breathless souls, husky voices,
Calming down, resuming breaths,
And slow embrace,
Souls,
Settle to embark, to set ablaze,
The timeless ardent sparks.....

If one day

I f one day
You set your sails toward other shores
With softer sands, smoother stones
I would not stop you
For you are a princess building castles
With my imperfect sand
I would not hate you
How can I hate the one
Who brought the sunlight to my shore

So if one day you change your sails
I will command the waves
To take you there
With my tears, I will flow you away
To your desires

But do not expect me to look back
Because I will not search for you

This part of the story is where you can forget
The shore that loves you
While I laugh at the sand castles
That you also left

Come a thousand sunrises and sunsets
Come heat, storm, and hail
Do not expect my hands to reach out to you

For even my feet will not move to follow your trail

Because...

Because my knees would be planted, heavily
Into the sand
Where you set your last footprint on my shore
Day and night, I will tell the waves how much I love you
With a hope that they would carry my message
To your new sand castles
And perhaps you would hear my heart echo
Behind your smile
As I go steep, down
To my neck, buried
In my own shore
While I stare at the horizon
And wait
For your return.

The Pleading

As I walk, on the beatific path,
My feet are caught and painfully restrained,
As I cry for help, I glance at the sky,
Oh I am the revered,
Of the Demon's eye;

I need you my Seer,
My Wizard, My God,
Pull me away,
From the Devil's clutch,
And relieve me of,
The throbbing stings,
This harrowing quelch!

Running Solitary

Perspiring and breathless,
Sniffing the humid sea breeze,
We jog, we talk, we laugh over sweet nothings,
I put my earphones on
For that latest song
As you snatch it from me
With raised eyebrows,
My irritation evident
You plant a kiss on my lips,
And there goes the agitation,
Lost in the sea gust;

I run and run,
And realise
I had been running alone,
And then a sudden gush of air
Storm the inside of me
My beloved
I love you for sending
Your kisses filled with your fragrance
As they find me running solitary
Across the oceans and the seas.........

I Adore You To Pieces

I adore you to pieces
With every drop
Of my soul, playing
With your fingers
Surrendering
Everything

I adore you to pieces
Perhaps not knowing
What love is
Except that
When you laugh
I breathe
And when you sleep
I dream

I adore you to pieces
With my unearthly body
From which arise, unearthly yearnings
That are out of bounds
Because I have heartbeats
That do not belong to me

I adore you to pieces
With my whole self
Fed
To your loin

And your domesticated body
Boned
By my thrusts

I adore you to pieces
Like a pagan who stands
Before the altar of his goddess
Sure of what I believe
I tear away my robe, I kiss your feet
And pray "Teach me to live"

Because I adore you
I adore you to pieces.
I need you to see me
I need you to see me as I am
Without rhetorical structures, devices, illusions
See me naked, raw and magic filled
With all my bones, aching
For your touch
Come with your fingers, ready
To pen new verses
Come ready to tattoo a novel
On my body
And teach me literature

And I will show you how spells can
command and bend your body
Manipulations of the blood, skillful uneven pressures
Magic mirrors made of sweat
As I whisper incantations down your skin, evoking
Rivers, gushing
From your pulsating loin, a flood

Of divinity, without you being touched
For you shall remain sacred as you are
Until you beg for more
And only then, will you forget how to walk

My Saint, I need you to see me
Because my life depends upon your eyes
And so do not think that I can leave you
Alone behind the tread
How can one live without fire
How can I live without your eyes
When in a world of lies
You are the only truth I know.

I Am Your Book's Last Page

I have been the last page,
Of that blessed book,
You began to read,
A long time ago,

I awaited the read,
The hour when you would,
Flip through me,
I, who felt like an unlettered page;

Engrossed you were,
In apprehending that came first,
Or Inquisitive you were,
Seeking me, your haven verso;

And the moment arrived,
When you resolved,
To end your read,
And you turned,
To the very last page;

I feel your eyes,
As they interpret my very self,
Word by word,
Like a colloquy,
Of the eyes with words;
And beatified I am,

I Do

Resurrected I feel,
As You resolve,
To be committed forever till infinity,
To me,
For I be your book's last page.

The Blood Moon....Your Message Of Love

Prophesies penned
  since a thousand decades,
That the Blood Moon would bring,
Cataclysm and alluvion,
Why?
I know not, neither do my heart,
Wishes to know!
Because,
For me, this beauteous astral luminescence,
The magnificent red,
Glowing like a million red roses,
Sprinkled with glitters and gleam,
Is a message from him,
Written with the ink of his soul,
"I adore you my Dear one,
I felt your tears in my eyes,
My heart ached with your heart in stings,
Weep no more, your pain isn't yours alone,
Let me walk along"
And I scribble my words on the beautiful Blood Moon,
"I miss you most today,
Come hither, hold my hand,
Let me forget my piqued heart,
In the warmth of your embrace"........

Poems are little accidents

Poems are little accidents on a paper
Sudden drops of ink on white pages
Like the accidental drop of a heart

And tonight is like all poems that I write to you
Where I stare at my heart, beating
On the paper
But like some strange discovery, I realize
It is not my heart
Because it is staring back at me
It is beating and I am watching
It is writing and I am reading

This is the accident
This is the accident

For knowing you, I am confronted with
a heart that cannot be tamed
For knowing you, it is falling off my table
To your lap of roses

And I cannot move.

From Across The Seas

The morrow breeze whispers, mumbles,
An epistle, your message,
From across the seas;

The first ray of the Sun
Brushes on my cheeks,
A touch of your palm,
From across the seas;

Heat of the noon,
Burns my frame,
It's your warmth,
From across the seas;

The rising dusk,
The twilight,
I feel the sighs,
From across the seas;

The midnight's moon,
Scatters it's luminescence,
Butterflies on my lips,
Its the kisses blown,
From across the seas;

The sleep, the repose,
Dreams of togetherness,
It's the spell cast on me,
From across the seas....

It's Beautiful

It's beautiful,
To fall in love with you,
Every passing moment,
To let the urges be on fire,
To let the heart play it's own songs,
The songs of longing,
It's beautiful,
To have found you,
To have discovered the rarest gem,
To have unsheathed the secret de amor,
It's beautiful,
To pen not pain
Not sorrows,
Not miseries,
But love and yearning,
Every passing day,
It's beautiful,
Our love, our togetherness,
That's one of its kind,
It's beautiful........

When I miss you

When I miss you, I do not search for you
I become still
Still as the night without stars
Still as the cold that muffles the voices of the grass

Sometimes I rise as a butterfly that
suddenly stops halfway in the air
Halted like a statue, my wings frozen
While everywhere, the butterflies land to kiss their flowers
I see them laughing, I see them smiling
Then I look at myself

Other times I stand alone on the shore
and throw pebbles at your window
Somewhere, out there, maybe I would hit it
But the sounds only bring more silence
And the silence only carries the restlessness of the waves

I can feel you from afar
Maybe laughing, maybe writing, maybe sleeping
Because when I miss you
I watch my soul jump off the cliff, repeatedly
As if looking for the right way to do it
And while the wind carries your breaths
The trees look at me with your eyes

And I am still ---
A dry leaf, falling
Waiting
For you to blow a kiss
To teach me how to live.

When Souls In Love Talk

E ver heard of two souls talk?
Well they do,
And this is how they converse,
When they are in love,
And the love,
Love, that is a gift from the verses:

"Oh love! I know not what to say,
I go weak with every word you express,
God! This is all that my lips can utter,
As my words loose themselves,
And in your eyes they sway."

"My Wizard, mention nothing,
Convey no words,
Respond not to my expressions,
Keep those phrases enclosed,
Say nothing,
Say no more,
Because when you utter nothing,
You say it all"

"My life you are,
Abandon me not,
Reckless my whole self would be,
I would forever be,
Callous and cold"

"Oh my enchanter,
Since that dawn when my words found you,
I am just a body,
As my soul resides in you with yours,
When you hold my hands,
I feel like the owner,
Of the planet of gold;
When your lips kiss mine,
I feel like a billionaire;
And when I am in your embrace,
I feel like the queen of Athens!"

"Oh my Poesy,
Take my entire self,
For nothing is mine now,
Every measure of me,
Is yours"

"I love you my master,
And can utter no more,
For my eyes are in tears,
And tears would say it all"

You've Won Me Again

Your words are like the arrows,
Arrows of raptures of love,
Overflowing with blissful zeal,
Like a sudden burst of a volcano,
A volcano of the white and pure,
Ashes of yearning,
And with your expressions,
You win me every time,
You've won me again........

Dear Chatterbox

Dear chatterbox finally i have this fleeting chance to talk i want to ask how are you but if i do i will not be able to continue so my dear chatterbox what im simply trying to say is that i believe in your words more than i believe in the bible even though you are sometimes unaware of the words that escape from your lovely mouth but nothing is ever wasted because i make an altar out of your voice in which i offer my soul to the infinite goddess in your eyes your words rain upon me like speeding bullets perfectly calibrated just for my ears and while between your high and low tones is my solitude between your lips and your voice is my dream ah my dream to hear your voice while i make mad love with your lips succulent and divine lips of honey lips of wine so intoxicating sweet is the joy of the moon but sweeter is the joy of having your mysterious thoughts reverberating in my body and your silly whispers resounding in my bones that the stars began to contemplate what happiness really is when they saw me listening to my chatterbox while smiling to the stretch of the sky and laughing with the light of the sun.

The Longing

The Longing,
    To see your angel face,
While you are asleep,
And I plead the night to pass,
In the most dawdling pace;

The Longing,
To see you wake up,
Open those eyes, the ethereal gems,
And look at me, as I stare at you,
Beseeching the moment,
To freeze;

The Longing,
To hold your hand,
As I bend closer,
To Kiss you on forehead,
And break the bewitching silence,
To say,
I Love You....

I Am Yours

When you stand in front of the mirror,
Your image you won't see,
As it would be none,
But a reflection of me,
And a proof it would be,
That yours I am,
I am yours,
Those bounds no one can invade,
Inside those bounds reside,
Our souls, yours and mine,
Forever and till eternity....

I carry your tears

I carry your tears
Wherever I go, whatever I do
I carry them with me
I hold them securely that no drop can fall
Thus you will not lose a tear
And I will not lose a part of you

But cry, my saint, cry if you should
And I will count the tears
Cry a river and flood the cosmos, even drown the gods
With tears of gems, all crystalline, raw and innocent
Cry

I understand...

Because I feel your pain in strings, sewn into my chest
Made of little blades mixed with shards
of glass, roughly stitched
They rub against my beating heart
That if only the stars could hear my burning sighs
The sound alone would make them weep
Weep with tears enough to flow
anything to the ends of the world
Enough to flow me to you

So cry, my saint, cry
And know that they are my tears
Because your tears cannot leave your eyes
Without leaving mine

Because I feel your tears
I carry them in my eyes.

Sometimes All I Wish

Sometimes all I wish,
Is to silently crawl,
And invade that beautiful mind,
And fathom,
What you think,
When you look at me,
With a tender gaze,
Delightful expressions,
And a smile,
That I would die for!

You Are My Salvation....

My beloved,
A prayer, a dream,
Your effort, my soul's joyous scream,
You whispered, I heard,
You played, I hummed,
I felt your fingers write verses,
On my uncovered skin,
While you dreamt of me,
From miles away;

Hey Wizard!
You know what....
My throat felt full with tears,
Some funny old astrologer said,
I won't live long enough,
But who wants to live long!
A moment of that glimpse,
Of your beaming smile,
A dive into the cherubic river,
That flows in your eyes,
A sublime touch of your hands,
On my dying frame,
And I would be liberated,
For, You my love,
Are my salvation........

You are divine

You are divine
I am not
Thus here I am to do my penance
With a stench of whisky on my lips, I now paint
my sins on the fragrant walls of your church
For I have come to set fire to your holiness
To give light to what is pure
You are divine
I am not
Now hear my prayers:

I pray for you, Dear One
And while I await for my prayers to sink into the ether
I adore you with my humble graces
Feel my hands confess to your skin, hungry for blasphemy
And while my conscience burns with your pious
lips, tell me the sciptures with your tongue
Mark them with crossfires on my body
Then wash me with your breaths while you
hide me inside the altar of your mouth
For I am only a sinner
Sincere to be cleansed

I pray for you, Dear One
See me with your open eyes
And find a man whose sins burn passionately for hell
Please save me with your most sacred sacrament

For I have another sin to tell
Then close your eyes
And I am there
A saint
Made by you

Have mercy
Have mercy
And hear my prayers.

Our Perennial Love

A midst those smirks and simpers,
Making its way,
through the crazy grins,
A cosmic union of two distant souls,
Is dawning;

Our verses are one,
So are our quintessences,
And our images are carved,
In each others hearts,
By those very modest grins;

Let me sculpt our moments,
Moments when we are apart,
Moments when we be one,
Into an immortal sculpture,

Or

Let me chisel our names,
On pebbles,
And stones,
And crystals,

Or let me just etch my heart,
In yours, My beloved,

We are no Apollo and Daphne,
Or Clytie and Helios,
We are You and I,
Striding on the maple sheathed path,
Of Our Perennial Love....

Waiting........Still

Ever been in a situation,
Where someone's absence takes over
Your thoughts, your imaginations?

Ever felt like a leaf,
That slowly goes brown from green,
For without water, it looses its sheen!

Ever wept,
For no apparent reason,
Like your heart is the atmosphere,
And there's a sudden change in the season!

Ever played the notes of wanting,
On the violin,
Where the bow speaks of the yearning?

Ever waited for someone,
Burning the midnight lamp,
Seeking something in the surrounding twilight?

I am all of this,
When I don't hear from you,
When I don't see you,
I am,
Waiting........Still.

The Gravity Of Your Love

My beloved,
Remember those golden lakes,
In which we used to sail,
In the boat of our dreams,
Rowing across the orchards,
Where the trees bore glittering gems,
You were a knight,
A princess I was,
And the first time I saw you,
I felt all yours,
I fell in love with you;

My love,
Remember that enchanted twilight,
When the invisible particles,
In the celestial sphere collided,
As it was the moment,
Of our souls' rendezvous,
And when I first read from you,
I felt all yours,
I fell in love with you;

My sweet,
Dream that blessed moment,
That would be,
Our beings' gratification,
Because then,

I Do

I would look into your eyes,
And fall for you again;

This is no momentary love,
No evanescent affection,
But my life,
It is what my soul feels,
It's the gravity of your love........

Only time

Only time keeps us apart
Days and nights are moving
I keep counting the sunrises
I keep staring at the moon
My lips search for your breath in the wind
By fate, I am sure, I will find it soon

Sometimes I count the waves and wonder:
If I follow your footprints in the sand
Will they lead me to your waiting arms?
If I follow your scent in the air
Will the stars conspire and take me there?

But like everything sacred, like everything worth seeking
I feel you here, I feel you everywhere
Like some phantom hand sweetly
plucking my heartstrings
Like some strange spell in the air
That my dreams leap alive with the
sunrise, I hear the stones singing
Then night comes, and the moon
looks at me with your eyes
Because you give meaning to everything
You give meaning to everything
Even your laugh defines my life

And because you are now a creature of magic

I Do

I dance in the rain, your wet kisses pouring
on my face, and all over my body
I smile, I sway
Knowing that you are only
A heartbeat away.

The Night's Mumbling Heart

If the nights could know,
The silent yearning
Of this soul in love,
There would be no dusk;

If the days could know,
The chaotic shrill,
Of this soul in love,
There would be no dawn;

My head would bow,
A million times,
To thank thee my Lord,
That You made the moon,
The stars, the sun and the breeze,
For these are the messengers of love,
There mere brush convinces my soul,
Into a temporal ease....

Lovers' Rhapsody

As I lie down on the snow,
Seduced by its beguiling white,
Freezing, cold, yet letting my body,
Be wrapped in its ivory smoothness,
It melts by the heat of my mortal frame,
Drop after drop,
it flows down from my cheeks to neck,
Caressing me with its cold touch;

My pen awaiting my command,
Rises to be embraced between my fingers,
As restless as my inner self,
To capture the serenity around,
In the most mesmerizing words;

I scrawl, my blissful spirit,
Sprinkled on paper,
But Oh, He espies me from afar!
I see you!
I see you my enchanter!
I see you behind that tall pine tree,
Your eyes occupied in composing,
Their own beauteous rhymes,
And we both write verses,
I write you on paper with ink,
While you write me,
In your imaginations with your eyes,

And so we become,
Two rhapsodists, making opus,
Embracing each other,
Through expressions, through words,
Through poetry, and through Nature.........

Our Voices

I am sloshed,
Inebiriated and laced,
In the saline froth,
Drunken with your thoughts,
Besotted by the sound,
Of your majestic voice;

I see those golden and orange rays,
Of the setting sun,
Like beauteous fire strings,
Dancing to the blazed beats,
Of my flaming heart,
A heart that's on an impetuous stride,
To be one with yours;

My inner self,
Listened to your impassioned voice,
The voice, that's the bow,
Which plays on the strings,
Of my heart, it's inflamed violin;

Can you hear the song love?
May be, a murmur!
Or a whisper?

Those are my breaths,
Brewed with the sound of my voice,

That is my song,
Which I filled up the setting sun's rays with,
So that they sheathe you,
The whole of you,
With the morning glow,
As they rise tomorrow,
In your hemisphere;

I wonder,
How else do I say,
I miss you!
Or
Should I just say
I miss you?

Our love

Our love is no less than the mountains and the
flowers
No less than a drop of soul in a wineglass
You drink me every time

Our love is as alive as the trees and the stars, laughing
Your existence is as the leaves in the forest
You are everywhere, I am anywhere
And I touch your essences, smooth as stones
While you hold me, with hands made of my bones
Our kisses fill each other, like how a river fills the ocean:
Kisses creating
Forever

How can one not love
Your beautiful mind?
How can I not love
How you love?

If beauty means anything to the world
Let it be so, let it be so
I have seen what I needed to know:
How my heart beats when you breathe
The endless sky in your eyes
That I kiss you

Under the light of your infinite stars
Tasting all my dreams
In the corners
Of your lips.

You, I And The String Of Pearls

There's a string of pearls,
Inside my heart,
Which binds it with yours,
And every pearl speaks to me,
As I miss you every hour;

"He's the one,
The one you sought,
Then what makes you,
Adrift in dismal thoughts?"

"Oh you beauty, You fair pearl
I miss him,
He be my heart's Duke, my earl!"

"My dainty lady,
He craves for you even more,
He sheds no tear,
But to lose you, is his biggest fear"

"I know my little snowy jewels,
But I know not how to rival this void,
Every particle of the universe,
In such moments, seem so cruel"

"Patience Oh our fair dame,
It would bear the sweetest fruit,
In his embrace you shall be,
You would soon be led,
To the beauteous true love's route"

"This ache, the wanting,
Denies me perseverance,
My body awaits it's soul,
And the devoir of him, is fiercely haunting"

Let Me...Let Me Be....

Let me,
Let me be,
Let me be the kind of lover,
Who cherishes your existence like a lunatic,
Like a stranded bigot,
Who has been abandoned long ago,
But finds her seeker out of nowhere,
You, who adores me like no one else do,
Whom I honor more than the Gods;

Let me,
Let me be,
Let me be the charm woven in a string,
Or an amulet or a talisman,
Wear me around you,
For I be your protector from the evil eyes;

Let me,
Let me be,
Let me be that unapologetic fool,
Who knows the intentions of the prying eyes,
But act innocent,
And be the sword to behead what holds,
Those snoopy minds;

Let me,
Let me be,

Let me be your armor,
And take every blow,
Every tempest,
That strides towards you;

For You,
You are mine,
Call me obsessed, or a maniac,
But this is what I am,
This is what I am when I love,
And the moment I met you,
Was the only moment I realized,
The unspoken definition of Love........

I Need You........

A re you asleep my beloved?
I know, to sleep has become,
Like the world's toughest task,
Shedding the imposed material masks
We both are now,
captives for lives,
In the ethereal prison of Love;

The confinement amidst,
Radiant blissful florets,
Efflorescence bestowed,
By abundance of adoration,
Plethora of passion,
And opulent dreams,
Where the springs of fervor,
Rise to flow towards the heavenly skies,
And the sorrows flow downstream;

Are you rejoiced my soul?
I know, the joys know no bounds,
But so does the longing sees no confines,
We are like two souls,
Thrilled and euphoric,
On discovering each other,
But so are we tearful and miserable,
As the distances are sometimes,
Far from bearable;

When the wolves of fate,
Dragged me downhill,
I was numb, numb with the pain,
I fell and strode ahead, fell, and climbed again,
Taking the filth and the waste,
Of the egoistic souls,
Made me overburdened,
And I slipped and fell more;
And just when I was,
To fall down the cliff,
Into the valleys of death,
You held my hand, and pulled me up;

I know not now,
How to walk alone,
I know not,
How to breathe without a purpose,
I know not,
How to survive without being loved,
I know not,
How to live without you my beloved;
So let me be straightforth,
And let me be true,
My seer,
You are all I have,
All that matters to me,
You are my world,
I see the unbound love in you,
So be mine,
You are the love I construe,
My soulmate,
I need you....

Little conversation

She: If the stars are so madly in love with each other
Why is it that they are so far apart?

He: Between two points, there are
an infinite number of points
Just as between two stars, there are
an infinite number of stars
We just do not see them from below

She: And so?

He: For one star to touch another
It has to collide with billions of stars

She: Hmmm...
Then why do stars don't do it?
Love is the greatest thing

He: In magic, it is called Respect
An immutable law of the universe
Often misunderstood

She: Respect?

He: Men have their laws which can easily be broken
But the universe has its own immutable laws
Otherwise all stars will fall

And no star will be left in the sky
Therefore to save nature
Love has to bend
Just as how stars cave in to darkness

She: Hmmm... But there is something
that you do not realize

He: What?

She: Stars are made of eyes
And stars always make love with their light

He: Very good... But you keep thinking about
stars that you just missed the whole point

She: What?

He: I am in love with you
And I will always be in love with you.

The Sound Of Your Voice

A helpless self,
Knowing not how to swim,
When half of me is in water,
And the other half,
On the brink to get whelmed,
Failing on my breaths,
Like dying a slow death;

Oh, this is my portrait,
When I don't hear from you,
For longer than what I can bear,
And My beloved,
I need to devour your voice,
Every second and everywhere,
Because it's not the air,
That keeps me alive,
But the sound of your voice........

All The Love Within Me

Love be my anthem,
Love's immersed in my soul,
With Love I am reborn,
Love makes me whole;

Love I do like never before,
In Love, my subconscious is lost,
In the glowing waters,
Of the desire filled shores;

Love is my gift,
Love I sought relentlessly.
Love is the end of my unfaltering journey,
Love is the air that lets my mortiferous self live;

Love is You,
You are me,
I am so absorbed into you,
All this to say my beloved,
For you, for you only,
There's All the love within me........

Our Voices, Our Lyrics, Our Odes

Words, expressions,
　　And the sprinkles of adoration,
A language, sui generis for love,
Whether it's my pen or yours,
Whether it's my verse or yours,
Whether those're my thoughts or yours,
They would always be.
Our confessions,
Of unceasing and boundless love,
That flows,
In every single tear we shed in yearning,
Every single epithet we write in longing,
And so my love,
Like our souls, that are one,
In a ceaseless and divine bond,
So are our verses, our lyrics, our odes........

Spells need energy

S pells need energy to be casted
If you take energy from the stars
The stars would lose energy
But nothing is really lost
Because nothing in nature can die
The energy taken from the stars
Only undergoes an alchemical transmutation
A divine change
Into the spell

It is a holy sacrifice

Accordingly, sometimes we need to give some energy away
To make the whole universe rise
Together, with our Will
And make dreams materialize
Otherwise, there will be meaningless collisions of galaxies
Rough stains on the ether

Thus, sometimes souls need to bend
And cave in like the stars
So the sky can keep its light
While the souls continue
To make love
Through the night.

I Have Loved You Since Time Immemorial

Seasons,
Numerous morning Suns,
Countless Starry nights,
Unquenchable Karmas and births,

I have loved you since time immemorial;

Braving the floods and torrents,
Counting all the shooting stars,
Searching and seeking,
Walking past the wild-woods and thickets,

I have loved you since time immemorial;

Faced a thousand deaths,
For a zillion times,
I stood at the gates of Heaven and Hell,
Only to be reborn,
And seek you again,

Oh my love.....

I have loved you since time immemorial,

To Love you till time immemorial.....

Wake Up, Good Morrow To You!

Wake up, Good morrow to you!
For you're to me,
The first ray of the morrow sun;

For I wish to see you rub those drowsy eyes,
And wake up from that soporific sleep;

I know the night was long,
Our frames were interlaced with each other, but not along;

You appeared in my gorgeous specter,
Even the rainbow smiled, spilling
upon me its seven colours;

The day be a special one, as you'd
soon hold a fraction of me,
The surface you would touch, bears my touch unseen,

So wake up,
From that sublime sleep,
It's the moment for us to meet........

Oh Mine........

O h mine,
Our love is like a necklace of pearls,
Lots of ivory whites,
Woven in the strongest of the strong thread,
The thread blessed by the heavenly bodies,
And all the Gods and Goddesses anyone ever knew of;

But the creator of this necklace, the Lord Himself,
Added few black stones too!
But Oh mine,
These tiny black gems are not the bad times,
But moments than He gave us,
To know how much we love each other;

Let there be any such hours of little discontentment,
I promise to take you out of the deepest of the dungeons,
I promise to love you more every passing moment,
I promise to fill our string with silver
and white and gold pearls,
I promise to stand besides you
whatever the situation may be,
Because Oh mine,
I,
Cherish you,
hail the showers of devotion upon you,
am the blessed in your embrace
relish the moments with you,

live in your soul,
zealously stand amidst the sorrows and You

Oh and did I tell you,
The storm has passed, and safe we are,
Together, forever........

Beneath The Moon....

In a chalice that glitters,
Radiant with the gleam of our souls,
Filled with the wine of eternal love,
In which we see our reflections together,
Let's sip on the heaven's ambrosia,
As I repose in your embrace,
Beneath the Moon........

Street rat

I am a street rat
A dirt in society...
What are my chances of winning her heart?
How can she even
See me?

From her golden castle she can view
Men with various dispositions
Few are wise, most are false, maybe some are true
Because this is the war of the night
This is plain darkness brooding in sight
Treacherous thieves, beguiling minds
Ready to snatch
My princess Beauty apart

O, gentle Moon, can she even see
the flowers in my mouth?
I wish to pass these to her, give everything to her
But with what light, what art, what tune?
Please tell me, sweet-gentle, gentle Moon

I have hands made for her cheeks
And nothing more but a lamp, with
a genie still under training
Yet the night is on, marching like starving ants
To eat her laughter away
Dazzled by her beauty, ready to slaughter

I Do

But if only she would look at me
As if I were made of silver stars
If only she would keep her eyes on me
And set fire to these haunted hours
Perhaps with one touch of her finger
Like a drop of her love, taken from the
depth of her eyes, black and deep
Then I would sing this night to stop
And forever
Sleep.

To Meet Thy Élan Vital

One step forth,
Few swim strokes,
Trespass through the woods,
Intruding haunted graveyards,
Where spirits roam sharp and shrewd,
Daring the cimmerian night,
When drooping,
It spreads its wings,
To take a hasty flight,
The cloudbursts drenching It down,
Now dragging for Its wings are soaked,
Almost there, there I can see,
There you stand,
As It wins the journey,
And holds your hands;

It.....

'It' is not a warrior,
'It' is not a knight,
'It' be my soul,
'It' be my subconscious self,
That leaves my mortal frame,
Every night,
To meet thy élan vital....

Us Together

O n the snow clad path
   With pine sheathed in white
On either side of the tramp
Let our fingers be entwined
As we walk holding hands
Let's pen the verses
That have never been written before
That would never be written
After us....
Verses taken from your mouth, cascading
Down to my hungry lips
Passion unsheathing passion
With tongues waging war against each
other, resounding among the trees
From restless yearnings, seized, a whole new paradise leaps
Stifling the darkness, and I drink you whole
While you drown me in your waterfall of desires
As to smother my breath, into the light of your eyes
Write
Write us down...
With our fingers entwined, and the seed
of faith clenched in our palms
Write not knowing where this walk can go
Write, with one pen, held by our hands, melting
The snow.

The Eloquent Dusk

Reposing on a stone bench,
Ruminating,
Engrossed in your thoughts,
I discern the fervent darkness rise,
As if guarding the fading daylight;

I feel like a charmer,
A conjurer,
That awaits her sibyl,
A clairvoyant who shall surmise,
And join back the pieces,
Of my diffused stars;

But look at the destiny's fortuitous spin,
A flame, alive with magic, held my soul,
And my soul felt the smile of win;

The elan vital,
It's powers are beyond any imaginations,
Above all creations,
It is sibylline in itself,
For it is our souls, the truly ours,
Which traversed across the material world,
Like a bee finding its way,
through the nectar's sweet fragrance,
Your soul sought mine, and mine, yours;

Had my soul not found yours,
Love would've been for me,
Just a bygone word;

Do I say 'Thank You',
Or should it be 'I Love You',
All I say, seems so less;

But the only truth I know,
Is that My being,
Is incomplete without you,
My soul flutters in pain,
Without yours,
I care not about the material world,
For the only world I know of,
Is You........

And so my day's colloquy with the dusk,
Comes to an end,
As I look forward,
To tomorrow's eloquent dusk....

Sweet Phantom Of The Night

Sweet phantom of the night
What matter are you made of?
You possess me as how fire is possessed by light
How can I move without knowing you?
How can I stop my breaths from reaching you?

I wander in the curvature of your eyes,
throwing pebbles at the moon
My dark maiden, you fill me with your rays
Like a basket of roses falling from heaven
Here I count your numberless graces
While my whole world depends upon your gaze

And because our love dances
Because our love sways
Beneath the endless sky
Our souls wet in the rain
Of kisses
Amidst the immense blackness
As the hue in your eye
My sweet phantom of the night, I
always move in your sight
While you, in mine
And this, my love, is sweet goodnight.

Perseverance En Amour

There you stand solo,
   On the white sands of a distant beach,
While I poise alone,
With my miserable heart,
In the porch facing the sea;

The saline breeze there sheathes you,
As the wind here caress my frame,

Letting the twilight pass,
Until the new dawn,
Fondled by,
Sprinkles and splash,
Of the rain and the drizzles,
I fear to leave the portico,
For I want not to be devoid,
Of that smallest particle in the wind,
And that tiniest drop of the rain,
Which has touched you moments before,
Feeling my silver skin;

With dewy eyes and heavy heart,
I wish I could be there,
We would sit in the night's cold sand,
My head resting on your shoulders,
Our bodies warm with the closeness,
With eyes closed,

Tuning into the accent of the waves,
We would let the briny whiff,
Whisk against our cheeks;

I am awakened, awakened he is,
By the knock of the merciless moments,
As we envisage the distances which be;

But comforted is my inner self,
When your fervor says to me,
"My beloved,
Let this be the hour,
Of the passionate union of our souls,
As that moment I can espy,
That time for our enamored oneness,
Is nearing from afar,
It's the endurance of two hearts,
The perseverance en amour"

You........

The wait....this enticing wait,
    Some sprinkles of perseverance,
And garnish of patience,
My daily meal, that satiates my soul,
Which yearns endlessly for you;

Splendid is the aura of this fervour,
That keeps us striding forth,
As we cover the immeasurable distances,
Which lie between us;

Words,
Words are our bodies' companions,
For our souls are already one,
We travel on the cart of expressions,
The verses, the Poesy;
Be our innumerable confessions;

Life's been such a futile existence,
Till that beatific moment,
When I finally discovered,
My purpose of being,
You..........
You were before I sought you,
You are when I found you,
And you would only be,

The beauteous reason,
Of my life,
For You, my beloved,
Are my life............

Let There Be No Regrets!

A mistake,
A part of the past,
A lapse, a blunder,
Which in the present,
Owns no space;

Heart is a tender being in itself,
That owes us no favours,
That we kill it with regrets,
And force upon it,
The feelings of utter anguish and demur;

The wrong steps in the past,
Are but our mind's misjudgements,
Or time's miscalculations,
Or simply the heart's erratic move;

Let not a rotten fragment,
Or a foul memory,
Affect the present,
Let not what's faux pas
Let not your qualms,
Be a part of what's beautiful,
Love,
It is innocent,
Angelic and pristine,
Let's not the self-reproaches,

sway around,
My beloved,
Do not regret, contrite not,
Let our souls play their part,
Let them savor their wedlock........

Beauty Is An Illusion

Beauty is an illusion
A million convulsing lights, cut
Into more illusions
Beauty of the eyes, Beauty of the nose, lips, breast, skin

Remove Beauty
And I will remove my eyes
Remove Beauty
And my hands will follow
Remove Beauty
And eyes, hands, everything, shall go

Because the eyes are also an illusion
Hands, also an illusion
Thus, nothing really goes away, nothing follows
Because everything outside of the soul
Is an illusion ---
Scattered reflections of the Divine
Eaten by Time

Because Beauty itself is an illusion
Even Time is an illusion
But Love is not

Thus, one day, the most beautiful woman
Shall lay her head on my arm
Her white flowing hair, surrendering

On her gown
With my hand, supporting
Her spine
And she may not see, but surely feel
The dream of all illusions
While I carry her down the aisle
To marry her again.

The Eternal Embrace

As you smile,
Oh that beam....
I see a million meteors,
Descending from the vast azure;

As you laugh,
The celestial sphere flares up,
Like a star stepping,
In the red giant phase;

A drop of tear,
On the corner of your eyes,
Leaves the clouds clamour, the deafening thunders,
In the twilight sky;

And Oh that mischievous grin,
Like a flash flood,
Of wanton teasing,
Sends the waves of zeal,
In my restless veins;

And Oh, You catch my gaze,
And I pose innocent and naive,
And then we cackle and giggle,
Only to find ourselves,
In each others,
Calming Eternal embrace....

The Whole Of You

Glitters and sheen I crave not for,
Amongst the riches, I don't desire to be,
Gems and material gleam,
Resources and wealth,
Don't interest me,
But,
Richest I yearn to be,
With abundance of your love,
Possessions that I pray for day and night,
Are your kisses your touch,
The look in your eyes,
Your voice, your verses,
I want to possess,
The whole of you........

Till Our Absolute Exultation....

All that existed,
Everything that subsists,
Moves in accordance with the pace of Time,
Time that was,
And time that is,
Has displayed the continuity,
Of the lives and deaths;

My struggles and searches,
Perpetual and amaranthine,
Which spurned to halt,
Suddenly presented,
With the light of the Divine;

The mirror had once shattered,
Its pieces, like an unsolvable puzzle,
I walked and I danced, my feet bled,
But least did I know,
Those weren't the sorrows immortal,
But the vicious storm,
That rises and flares,
Just afore a euphoric rapture;

I met you,
Yes,
The hour of my beatific bliss,
The hour of my proven being,

The hour when my destiny flipped,
The hour of my mysticism elated;
When the meaningless turned sensible,
Worthless turned precious,
Abandonment into acceptance,
Futile into the substantial,
Barren into fruitful;

Such is the aura of your presence my beloved,
Such is the emission of the energy,
That surrounds you,
And accepts none, but me;

Let's rise,
And be on the elemental journey,
When I shall see you, without seeing you,
When I shall touch you, without touching you,
When I shall hear the beat of your seraphic heart,
That would be the moment,
Of my beatific triumph,
Till the moment,
Of our absolute exultation....

Powerful Spells

The most powerful spells
  Come in the form of prayers
Not with force nor conceited demands
Casters must not tie a leash and
drag the elements headlong

Because true incantations of the soul
Must be spoken
In silence
In love, without pride
Without hate
Only then will one's prayer have
The inertia of the entire universe

I remember how
My feet grew roots into the core of the earth
My breaths became the wind
And I sweat fire
I became a mere instrument
A wonderful instrument that the universe used
To cast the spells ---

Miracles, unfolding
Everywhere

And now you hold this instrument in your hands
Please pluck my rusty strings
And play.

Wishing My Enchanter....
A Happy Birthday!

I wish,
I could see you blow the candle,

I wish,
I could see you make a wish,

I wish,
I could offer you
That first piece of cake that I made,

I wish,
I could hear you praise,
Calling it the most delectable cake,
Oh but it's different,
My first bite would confess.
"Lady! It's the most unpalatable bakes!"

I wish,
I could see you,
Bearing the chatterbox that I am,
Pleading me after much poise,
"Oh my blabbermouth beloved,
Please lend me a moment to speak!"
And finally sealing my lips,
With the most passionate kiss!

I wish.......
These endless wishes for us,
Come to life someday,
And if,
You suddenly turn around today,
With a whisper echoing in your ears,
It would be my ardour,
Saying,
"Thank you for being born,
On this very day,
As your existence marks mine,
If you are, I am,
If you aren't, Nothing would be,
Here's wishing my enchanter,
A happy birthday...."

When We shall Meet....

Sitting solitary in an urban cafe,
Wooden ceilings and glass walls,
The planchments so breathtaking,
As if straight out of the forests,
My gaze discovers out of nowhere,
It's own engrossing theme,
A pathway,
Numerous striking blocks of concrete,
Alluring to my tired sight,
But,
My beloved,
To my love smitten eyes,
These are not merely the cement blocks,
To me,
These are like our moments,
Well planned by our destiny;
The pedestrians,
Walking on these blocks,
Are like the rough moments,
That we face,
During our charismatic adventure of togetherness;

I write these words, sipping my favourite hibiscus tea,
Taking off my wrist watch, I keep it in front of me,
Soon to find my thoughts abruptly diverted,
Enticed by the ticking of the second hand,
Moments bygone and hours passing,

Falling short of breaths, life decreasing,
And the only thought accompanying it,
Is that instant,
That second,
When being alive would be accomplished,
When we shall meet.........

If

If
You ask me
To write
A verse
For you
I will not tell
How the stars
Leap
To your eyes
Not about the moon
Breathing
On your skin
Nor the curve
Of your hands
Where the whole world lies

Because
The angels
Will only think
That I am mad
Writing drunk
Writing bad

Thus...
If
You ask me
To write

A verse
For you
This is how
It will be:

With my lips
Tracing poems
On the canvass
Of your body.

Steps To Thee....

With much Joy,
    And elated glee,
I greet the Twilight,
For a new day would dawn,
And so would another dusk,
As they are not
Just the days and the nights,
But the steps of the ladder,
Which lead me to thee................

Today And Every Morning....

Curled up in the bed,
Nestled in the wrinkled sheets,
Awaiting to be submerged,
In the love's rapturous beads,
I hear your voice,
Like a song in my ears,
And I open my eyes,
Oh but, you're not here!

So I write this song,
That I've been humming all along,
In the dreams and through the night,
As I imagine and I fantasize,
Flames burning,
As I wake up in your arms,
Today
And every morning;

So come now,
And fabricate all my barren dreams,
Let's flow together,
In the fancy streams,
So hold my hand,
And never give up on me,
And we shall rise together,

Today
And every morning,
Today,
And every morning........

The Seeker Of The Seer....

I know not since how many lives and deaths,
I wandered hither, thither,
Searching endlessly,
Without even the faintest signs of you;

I know not how many lives and deaths,
I have lamented and shed the tears of blood,
While I found nothing, no trace of you;

I have passed the births after births,
I was a reptile, a mammoth, a bird,
But soon the drop of mercy,
The Almighty fed me with,
To be born a human, and He said in blessings,
"Thee shall now stride,
On the final seeking ride,
Thou shall find what thou sought,
No more trials of fate,
No more blows of failures,
But a beauteous pearl,
Blessed be, the daughter of Love";

The holy sacrifice,
I shall make no more,
Enough of painful seeking,
My soul has suffered it all,
Love, is no cow, no goat,

Nor is it a human,
Whom one shall sacrifice;

Love, My Almighty told,
Is but a precious pearl,
A pearl so white and pure,
Which knows not what is life,
Or anger or greed or hatred,
Love knows love,
Love resides in the soul,
Love seizes the soul,
Soul possesses the Love;

I've found you after,
Precious lives in prayers,
Innumerable endurances,
When I died a birth of atrocious deeds,
I suffered the serpents' stings,
Which ruled the dungeons of hell;

Tell me Oh my Soul,
My beloved, my seer,
How else must I express?
Let me offer you,
My head, my life, my heart,
in a cuauhxicalli,
Choose one or take all,
And slain it with the sacrificial sword;

I am that treasure hunter,
Who found the rarest gem,
A gem that is my pride,

My joy and my reason to breathe,
For thy love,
To every living soul,
I can turn into a bundle of lies,
Let me be the sinner,
Or be punished in furnace,
If that is how,
You would be my paramour;

My dearest,
Let there be no looking back,
Let's just walk ahead,
With heads held high,
In Love,
For I have no strength to be,
The seeker of the seer again,
Because I know it's you,
It's only you....

There Is A Rose

There is a rose
In a faraway land
That writes and sings
She talks to the moon at night
While she flutters her invisible wings

That rose is far from anything
Even eccentric in many ways
Strange as a lone wolf dancing on the shore
With the purest smile on her face

I already met a hundred roses
Even swallowed a garden of petals
But only that distant rose of my desire
Has held my heart
With music, magic, and fire.

Shilpa Sandesh & Charlz dela Cruz

Cupid's Delight

She plays, hums and she sings,
The tunes of seraphic hymns,
Fingers on the frets,
Pneuma reaches the alpine heights,
Against the destiny and karma,
Conscience wins the fight,
And in the lustrous Heavenly beam,
She becomes the Cupid's delight....

Our Castle In The Air....

It's a beautiful home,
That we've built,
Where I step in as your bride,
Years of giggles and joy,
Few strides on the rough roads,
And here we're,
Let me show you our home........

That be the cubbyhole,
Of our little ones,
With the colours of pink and blue;

And that one, facing the sea,
Be our atelier,
Splendid with lots of hues;

There's our garden and greens,
Our vision of laughter and gleams,
Where barefoot we shall walk,
As the grasses tickle beneath our feet,
Our little bundle of joys,
Fill the air with joyous chirps and shrills,
As a solitary moment, a retreat,
Playfully, we together seek,
I feel my lips stretch, to give the widest smile,

As it's the home I envision,
Our abode it be,
As I am the everyday creator,
Of our castle in the air........

Mysticism

A volcano of elements,
　Sets me within me,
Ablaze,
With the sparks unknown,
Let everything be left behind,
Let nakedness be sheathed in white,
As the body sways,
In rhythm, rhythm of the chants,
The flute, a faint flute,
Hands spread, palms dancing in whirls,
Fingers stiffen,
The moon washes my bare self,
light permeating every pore.
Eyes of chimera conquer the material eyes,
The frame, pirouetting,
As my rob whirls and purls,
I am no more,
Materialism lynched by esoteric,
Quietism pulls me,
Mysticism dwells, as here,
As there, as everywhere,
I whirl in profound bliss,
submitted,
Till I drop,
Hushed by the presence unknown,
Lifeless,
I drop,

....

And My returning breaths,
My reconstructing pulse,
Croons the mantra,
Your name....

How Your Body Moves

How your body moves
From head to toe
Is like the wonder from ages ago
When goddesses roamed the earth and played with fire
Except that you play with stars ---
Stars in surrender to your open arms
Together with my heart

The skin of my dreams, my wishes bound
To your flesh
My prayer resounding from the ground:
'How do lips meet, and tongues mesh?'
Because you give new meaning to everything
Come immense nights, divine days
A touch is no longer a touch
A hug ceases to be just an embrace
I see souls
I see fire

Invaded by your esoteric existence, my
pores breathe invisible kisses
I even feel your tears on my cheeks
And your sighs leaving my mouth
How can this be? How can this be?

How do you move --- move me?
That I want to lick your wounds
I want to kiss your scars
And dream between your hands.

One More Day

One more day has passed,
   Some more moments have bygone,
All my eyes yearned for,
Is a sight of you,
All my arms crave for,
Is to take you in their embrace,
But joyous I am for the time that's past,
Because only now,
Our moments of togetherness shall come..........

Pain....

Pain.......
Like walking upon,
The path,
Sheathed by thousands of burning embers,
When the walk halts,
In the middle of the path,
And the frame melts,
Till the body itself becomes it's part

Pain........
Born, pampered,
A step on the sword,
Bruised and bled,
And now, hanging amidst,
Integrity and Love

Pain.......
The sudden shower,
Of abundance of adoration,
Passion I never knew,
When happiness knew no bounds,
The sudden blow,
My body pierced,
By the uninvited arrow

Pain........
Sobs know no bounds,
Tears are tired too,
Dried upon my cheeks,
What am I now to you?

Pain........
A bird flying in the widespread sky,
Joyous as it approaches
Its long sought destination,
And the huntsman called fate,
Shoots the bird down,
It's not dead, it just lost it's wings,
Be happy bird, you're still breathing
What else do you want for life!
You are still breathing!

Pain........
A blank page,
Scribbled upon,
Crumpled, torn,
And thrown,
Caught by the wind,
And to the lands of love,
It was blown,
Till it flew over the sea,
And a wave washed it away,
To the depths unseen

Pain........
My fingers ache,
But heart doesn't stop,

As love,
Is an ever burning flame,
Oh but,
This pain........

My Spell....

The words come together,
Verses are born,
Verses fall in love,
Spells are born,
Let me turn my name,
Into that voodoo chant,
Which when cast upon you,
Togetherness,
This destiny would grant,
So as you say my name,
And as you read my words,
When conscious,
Or when in Trance,
I am at that moment,
With your name on my lips
Doing the moon dance,
With the eyes of my imagination,
Gazing you from afar
My beloved,
Under my spell you are......

Laugh

Where does laughter go
        When it leaves the mouth?
How do you
Take it back?

Last night, I was at the mental hospital
Writing poems for you on the walls
Doctor said 'You are crazy!'
He was funny, so I laughed
Right there and then, he told everyone I can go

Because I laugh like mads among the stars
Although my own laugh pains my ears
But still I laugh endlessly
Butterflies, pixie dusts, falling on my lips
Erratic heart, skipping beats
While my soul
Floats
To the blues, with the wind
And the music
Of the Moon
This is the mystery
Of insanity

Because pure laughter is the sound of love
Once it leaves the mouth
I cannot pull it back

It is a one way ticket to your ears
And so I laugh
I laugh so beautifully
Only because you laugh
You laugh with me.

As Long As The Night Sways....

....S tay.....Stay by the window....
The Moon whispers,
Till the dawn rises,
Till the dusk vanishes,
Stay........
These stars are forming a bow,
A path so virile,
Step onto the curve of dynamism,
Hearken the sound of the wind,
Conceive the images,
That the passing clouds design,

For
The Stars are the flowers,
He sent for me

The wind is the words,
He conveys to me,

And
The clouds are the verses,
He writes for me..........

And so I stay..........
I stay by the window,
As long as the night sways....

Your Verses....
Your Words....My Eyes

Your verses,
  Your words,
Your unbound expressions of love,
My wizard,
You present me your heart,
In a golden platter,
And as my eyes capture the beautiful diction,
And your declaration of your love for me,
Amazed I am,
As I can see myself therein,
I blush, and feel like that velvet rose,
The petals of which,
A prince would kiss,
And it would turn into a princess,
With that true love's caress of the angelic lips,
So the emperor of my heart and soul,
These eyes await hither,
To embrace that verse,
Which be the spell,
To bring you here,
And let my petioles be touched,
By your warm quivering lips,
And turn me into your empress,
That destiny wants me to be........

My Precious....Good Morning To You!

The Good Morrow's sun is here,
 Saying 'come again' to twilight,
I slept like a baby,
In your arms, while you held me tight;
Even though I knew you're not here,
But I felt the touch of your soul,
Colossal is our love,
Rising high like gigantic Mount Elbrus,
Behemothic like the vast Pacific seas,
So here's the aurora's kisses,
Hugs and fervor's bliss,
To drench you in my love,
As you open your eyes,
Good morning to you!
My precious I love you,
Good morning to you.....

Before there were flowers

Before there were flowers
There was the fifth element traversing the open sky
Not knowing what happiness is, not
knowing what beauty is
It came like a lost wind merely passing by

Filled with dark matter, it knew no
peace, no rest, no songs
And it only inhaled its own burning sighs

Then after a million births and rebirths
Its longing found its body in my blood
I carried it in my chest, beating
Void, empty, bids of goodbyes
Until you were its vision
Only then did it genuflect, to meet your eyes ---
Eyes that talk, eyes that sing
Eyes of dreams, eyes that reveal
Where true love lies

At once, music filled the air, in perfect notations
Swarms of baby angels swooped in
And everything came to life
As you picked me up and raised me high

Above the clouds, past the stars
Into the blinding brightness of your eyes ---
And we breathed

Flowers.

A Song For You....

There's been,
A bit of a misunderstanding,
There's been,
Just few misconceptions,
But Oh my love,
My virtuoso and the gem of my eyes,
Love is but meant to be,
A brew of strife and glee,
So hold my hand,
And look into my eyes,
Tell me what you see,
It's you, isn't it?
It's you, yes it is!

It rained that night,
There were storms of fright,
When I craved for you,
To be held so tight,
So hold my hand,
Let's sail on the seas,
Of countless dreams,
The dreams that we've,
Woven together,

The dreams that we shall live,
The dreams that we would live.......

Listen to me hum,
As I sing this song for you,
I sing this song for you....

Would You Stay With Me Still?

S hort-lived are these blossoming hair,
And this fresh and blooming skin,
There would be a day,
When wrinkles and tiredness,
To my frame, the time would bring;

Grey-haired I would be,
And I might be impaired,
May be I would be,
Unable to walk myself,
Without you being here;

I might loose some memories,
That my soul vowed to treasure,
I may be like a puppet,
With it's strings in the hands of fate,
It might make me fall,
It might raise me high,
Of the clock's wrath I am not sure;

But in any of these,
Plays of life Oh Love,
Bear would you my fate's share,
Or would you be tired of it all?
Please don't abandon me,

For I have loved you evermore,
Even if my mind suffers forgetfulness,
My soul and body would always be yours,
Be with me,
Don't leave me,
Be with me,
To stay forevermore,
So tell me will you,
Would you stay with me still?
Would you stay with me still!

How do I appease your beauty?

How do I appease your beauty?
I pleaded you to come gently, touch slowly
Instead you came like a tidal wave
and obliterated everything
Merciless Glamour, what wrong have I done to you
Why did you enter my pores and consume my sanity
Why did you put the sun in my body
and the moon beneath my skin
That I have faeries dancing, playing
Deep within

And now my whole life is standing before me
Beautiful sins stirring my blood, erupting
Crimes of the flesh, rituals of the soul --- sweet to touch
Yet I do not ask for forgiveness
Not from your eyes that speak and grab
Nor from your hair, nose, or lips of fire and dreams
I do not ask for my confessions to be heard

How can I ask
When you continue to smother my breaths with
your silver tongue, feeding me a thousand secrets
That my hands are clenching the
stars and the boundless sky
With my soul leaving my mouth, praying
To join your precious sigh

I Am Restless

I know not,
Why this restlessness,
Is encompassing the inner me,
All my heart can cease,
Is that, it misses the voice of thee,
This stride I know,
Is a tumultuous one,
It calls for a patient walk,
It favors no hasty run;

But,
I am still consumed,
By this restlessness,
Never did I know,
To settle my inner self,
Would be like heart and soul,
In a row;

I feel at peace, but I am not,
It is thy need, a compulsion,
It's our destinies' most beauteous plot;

I am restless still,
The nerves in my head,
Seem hysteric too!

Your breaths flow in my veins,
But without you close to me,
They are jittery and fretful;

I am restless,
At this moment,
I know no patience,
No perseverance I acknowledge,
Tell me what is endurance,
Or courage or persistence!

Turbulent I feel,
I am restless........
Fitful I am,
I am restless........

Together Forever

You be the zephyr,
    While I be the twig,
In awe of your drift,
As you lift me,
From my dolorous being,
And take me along in your flux,
To the uncharted lands,
Of jillion blessings,
And measureless love,
Where you would be the Adam,
And I be your Eve,
Where there will be no Satan,
To send us on the journey of seeking,
That we've suffered for births;

And then we would be,
Untouched by the karma,
Guarded by the angels,
Never to be parted,
And to stay,
Together forever!

My Wizard....

I came into this world,
Like a wingless bird,
You gave me strength to fly,
Through the oceans and windy swirls,
I have been in love with you,
Since the Adam and Eve were cursed,
I will love you till,
Eternity.....
Till........
Infinity.......
And I will wait for you,
On the cold Sands of,
The beach in our dreams....

I Do....

M oon:
Beneath the tabernacle,
Of the sky veiled in stars,
Cupid be the Magic's best-man,
And Psyche, Poetry's bridesmaid,
With the holy book of the Poetic Spells,
You, Magic,
Under the laws of heaven,
The Hellenic Gods and Goddesses
Do you accept Poetry,
As your soul mate for life?

I do.

You, Poetry
Do you submit to all the spells and curses of Magic
And give to him your whole heart, body, mind, and soul?
And like the blood that surrenders to your veins
So shall you surrender to all his urges
Under the laws of Heaven and Hell
All Gods and Goddesses as above, so below
Do you accept Magic
As your soul mate for life?

I Do

I do,

To all your divine enchantments,
To all your beatific spells,
Like a falling meteor that surrenders
To the laws of gravity,
Like a nectar, that serves itself,
To the delightful lips of a butterfly,
With the blessings of the Gods and Goddesses,
As above, so below,
I submit my whole self,
To your beguiling raptures, my Magic,
I accept you as my soul mate for life!

Moon:
Under the enthralling submissions,
And the endearing obedience,
Underneath the innumerable dawns and twilight,
And the immortal Universe,
I now pronounce you,
Magic and Poetry,
As Soulmates for this life,
And all the future lives........

Printed in the United States
By Bookmasters